INTRODUCTION

When faced with money problems, difficulties with people, challenges at work, or just the busyness of life, your focus might not be as sharp and your resolve not as strong. Even though you go through the motions of your weekly routine without much notice from friends and family, you know deep inside that *life* is getting the best of you.

Jump-Start Your Christian Life: Five Simple Ways to Refresh, Restore, and Reset is written as a recharge for your Christian life. Through five simple principles, you can experience the boost you need to help you refresh, restore, and reset your life in godliness.

Regardless of whatever situation you might find yourself in today, *Jump-Start Your Christian Life: Five Simple Ways to Refresh, Restore, and Reset* can provide you with the information you need to refocus and strengthen your resolve. May these five simple principles radically energize your life as a Christian. God bless.

CONNECTION POINTS

When your car battery is too low to start the engine, one of the first things you might try is jump-starting the battery. In order to jump-start your battery, you'll need good connection points from an external source. A battery from a running car can provide the connection you'll need to give your car a quick power boost to possibly start your car. As Christians, we too need our connection points.

I am the true vine, and my Father is the husbandman. Every branch in me that beareth not fruit he taketh away: and every branch that beareth fruit, he purgeth it, that it may bring forth more fruit. Now ye are clean through the word which I have spoken unto you. Abide in me, and I in you. As the branch cannot bear fruit of itself, except it abide in the vine; no more can ye, except ye abide in me. I am the vine, ye are the branches: He that abideth in me, and I in him, the same bringeth forth much fruit: for without me ye can do nothing.—John 15:1–5

The first connection point you need as a Christian is Jesus. In John 15:1–5, Jesus states that He is the true vine and His Father is the husbandman (or vinedresser). In order to bear fruit, you, as a branch, will need to abide in Jesus because you cannot bear fruit on your own. In order to abide in Jesus, you would need to stay in a given place or state; to dwell, remain, stay, or tarry.[1]

If you want to continually abide in Jesus, you must pay close attention to what you think, watch, listen to, where you go, and what you say. You must also consider any influence your friends, family members, and associates might have over you. Some of these can seem harmless, but they can quietly separate you from your connection to Jesus. Because of the importance of abiding in Jesus, you might have to make some tough decisions on what you might need to remove from your life. This is part of your pruning process.[2]

Your second connection point is the Bible. As Jesus spoke to His disciples, He told them that the Word He spoke to them made them clean. In like manner, reading, studying, and meditating on the Bible will cleanse and sanctify you.[3] The Bible will shape your life in godliness and keep you on a path of righteousness.[4]

BLESSED 1

Blessed is the man that walketh not in the counsel of the ungodly, nor standeth in the way of sinners, nor sitteth in the seat of the scornful.—Psalm 1:1

The first Psalm begins with three ways a person can be blessed. Being blessed in this instance is defined as happy, and a happy person is someone who has a feeling of or shows pleasure or contentment.

1. A blessed person does not walk in the counsel of the ungodly. If you want to be blessed, acting on advice from ungodly people will not help you. Ungodly people have very few boundaries or limits on their thoughts or behavior—they're ungodly. Most often, they'll operate in any manner necessary to get their way, regardless of

who or what is impacted. They might even purposefully provide counsel contrary to your beliefs just to see you act out of character as a Christian.[5]

Seek out godly people who will provide counsel that will keep your heart, soul, and mind abiding in Jesus. These individuals will typically provide references from the Bible or some other aspect or reference of godly character or conduct.

2. A blessed person does not stand in the way of sinners. Standing is not only for being among a group of people in a specific location but also for taking a stance in attitude or behavior. First, if you choose to stand (or remain) among sinners and choose not to remove yourself from their company, you'll be in danger of being influenced by their behavior.[6] Second, you can also have a stance in attitude or behavior similar to sinners. This stance might not be influenced by any other person—just your own sinful desires.

Blessed people don't stand in the way of sinners. They take a stand against them.[7]

3. A blessed person does not sit in the seat of the scornful. Like sitting in the way of sinners, sitting in the seat of the scornful works in the same manner. As being scornful is mocking, ridiculing, or scoffing at someone, you can be seated among people mocking, ridiculing, or scoffing at others, or you could be the one mocking, ridiculing, or scoffing.

When some people think of mocking, ridiculing, or scoffing, they might think of some loud, boisterous person yelling at people, but this isn't always true. Some instances occur through subtle sarcasm and other verbal jabs among family members, friends, coworkers, and strangers. What might seem like harmless banter could be preventing you from not only being blessed, but also abiding in Jesus and growing as a Christian.[8]

Blessed people will not mock, ridicule, or scoff at people. They use their words to build up, encourage, and speak life into others.

GLORY   2

Whether therefore ye eat, or drink, or whatsoever ye do, do all to the glory of God.
—1 Corinthians 10:31

Many Christians separate various aspects of their lives like train compartments. One compartment might represent their home life; another compartment is for work; and another is for church, and so on. And if you think about it, you might act a lot differently in your work environment than you would at home, church, or among friends. In some compartments, you care what people perceive you to be, and in others, you could care less.

However, only one rule should exist among your life compartments. Though you engage different groups of people in each compartment of your life, your attitude and behavior should remain the same, to the glory of God.

So how can you glorify God in each compartment of your life?

Glory is defined as magnificence, excellence, preeminence, dignity, grace, or majesty.[9] Whether you are eating or drinking, in whatever you do, you should do it in a manner that brings magnificence, excellence, preeminence, dignity, grace, and majesty to God.[10]

Each day, and in every moment, you have an opportunity to glorify God. Glorifying God is not only about what you might do in or for your church. Whether you're driving on the road, dealing with difficult bosses, or facing heartbreaking situations, you can glorify God through your conduct. It's your opportunity to help others acknowledge the magnificence, excellence, preeminence, dignity, grace, and majesty of God.[11]

Ye are the light of the world. A city that is set on an hill cannot be hid. Neither do men light a candle, and put it under a bushel, but on a candlestick; and it giveth light unto all that are in the house. Let your light so shine before men, that they may see your good works, and glorify your Father which is in heaven. —Matthew 5:14–16

PRAYER 3

In its simplest form, prayer is your communication with God, a request for help (for yourself and others), an expression of thanks addressed to Him, or an object of worship. As you're encouraged to pray often,[12] Jesus has provided instructions on how to pray:

1. Do not pray to be seen by others.

And when thou prayest, thou shalt not be as the hypocrites are: for they love to pray standing in the synagogues and in the corners of the streets, that they may be seen of men. Verily I say unto you, they have their reward.
—Matthew 6:5

People who pray to be seen by others are considered as hypocrites. They're hypocrites because their true focus isn't in receiving an answer to their prayers or the people they're praying for, only the reward of recognition, which Jesus said they would receive.

2. Go to a private place.

But thou, when thou prayest, enter into thy closet, and when thou hast shut thy door, pray to thy Father which is in secret; and thy Father which seeth in secret shall reward thee openly. —Matthew 6:6

In comparison to those who pray openly to be seen by others, enter a private place to pray in secret. What the Lord sees in secret, He will reward openly.

3. Keep your prayers simple and to the point.

But when ye pray, use not vain repetitions, as the heathen do: for they think that they shall be heard for their much speaking. Be not ye therefore like unto them: for your Father knoweth what things ye have need of, before ye ask him. —Matthew 6:7–8

Do not be like the heathens (pagans, sinners) who pray with vain repetitions. Those who pray in that manner believe they'll be heard because of their repetitions and long prayers. Jesus says not to be like them because your Father already knows what you need.[13]

4. Pray after this manner (or fashion):

Our Father which art in heaven, Hallowed be thy name (Matthew 6:9).

As you enter into prayer, begin by acknowledging your Father in heaven. Hallowed (holy, set apart) is His Name. Your heavenly Father is to be honored, worshiped, and revered.

Thy kingdom come, Thy will be done in earth, as it is in heaven (Matthew 6:10).

Pray for the Kingdom of God to come and God's will to be done in earth, as it is in heaven. In heaven, there's obedience to God, along with holiness, honor, worship, and reverence.

As Jesus said the Kingdom of God is within you, in your heart,[14] you too have the ability to live in conformity to God's will.[15] As you pray for God's Kingdom to come, you're asking for His Kingdom to be advanced in you and in others around the world by His Spirit.

Give us this day our daily bread (Matthew 6:11).

Each day, you're asking for the substance that's required for that day and not the next day or week. This is evidence that this prayer is to be made daily—trusting God as your provider.

And forgive us our debts, as we forgive our debtors (Matthew 6:12).

Ask God to forgive you for your sins only as you forgive those who sinned against you. Holding onto unforgiveness for any reason can have eternal consequences:

For if ye forgive men their trespasses, your heavenly Father will also forgive you: But if ye forgive not men their trespasses, neither will your Father forgive your trespasses. —Matthew 6:14-15

Lead us not into temptation, but deliver us from evil: For thine is the kingdom, and the power, and the glory, for ever. Amen (Matthew 6:13).

You can ask God not to lead you into temptation. If times of temptation do come, the

Lord will show you a way of escape.[16] He will deliver you,[17] but you must be willing to turn from the temptation and take the path He shows you.

At the conclusion of your prayer, you acknowledge the Kingdom (rule), power (ability), and glory of your Father in Heaven... forever. Amen (so be it).

DELIGHT   4

Delight thyself also in the LORD; and he shall give thee the desires of thine heart.—Psalm 37:4

To delight in something is to take great pleasure or find something to be desired. Though Psalm 37:4 identifies a *benefit* in taking great pleasure in the Lord, many people struggle between delighting in themselves and delighting in the Lord.

1. The delight of self-indulgence. The delight of self-indulgence is pleasing one's self with whatever would make him- or herself happy. The origin of such desires can be found in Adam and Eve.

When the Lord created the heavens and earth, He dressed and arrayed them according to

His good pleasure. The man was created out of the dust of the ground and the woman out of one of man's ribs. She was created as a help meet to share in a common purpose to be fruitful, multiply, replenish the earth, and subdue it and to have dominion over the fish of the sea, the fowl of the air, and over every living thing that moves upon the earth.[18]

Adam and Eve had everything they needed. Their provisions were met. Their place of residence was dressed by the Lord.[19] They lived without the knowledge of good or evil. They had communion with the Lord in the garden. They lived without shame.[20]

During an encounter with the serpent, Eve was tempted to eat from the tree of the knowledge of good and evil. God commanded Adam not to eat the fruit from this tree, for if he did, God said he would surely die.[21] However, when Eve saw that the fruit was good for food, pleasant to the eye, and able to make her wise, she ate the fruit and gave some to Adam, opening their eyes to the knowledge of good and evil.[22]

Through this one decision of self-indulgence, Adam and Eve exchanged their delight for the Lord for a delight in themselves. Now, because of Adam's disobedience, every person after him would experience this same desire of wanting to please him- or herself.[23]

2. The delight of the Lord. In Psalm 37:4, David revealed a delight beyond self-indulgence, a delight in the Lord. When you delight yourself in the Lord, you take great pleasure in Him and find Him to be your ultimate desire. You want to spend time with Him in prayer, meditate on His word, fast unto Him, and live before Him in a pleasing manner.

Delighting yourself in the Lord is an intentional, all-consuming purpose that encompasses who you are as a Christian. Delighting in the Lord is not a condition for getting what you want in self-indulgence because the Lord becomes everything you desire.

A person who delights in the Lord is one who desires Him above all other things.

LOVE 5

Then one of them, which was a lawyer, asked him a question, tempting him, and saying, Master, which is the great commandment in the law? Jesus said unto him, Thou shalt love the Lord thy God with all thy heart, and with all thy soul, and with all thy mind. This is the first and great commandment. And the second is like unto it, Thou shalt love thy neighbour as thyself. On these two commandments hang all the law and the prophets.—Matthew 22:35–40

As you consider what it means to love the Lord with all your heart, soul, and mind, consider these definitions of love, heart, soul, and mind:

Love: an intense feeling of deep affection

Heart: regarded as the center of a person's thoughts and emotions; the central or innermost part of something

Soul: a person's moral or emotional nature or sense of identity; the essence or embodiment of a specified quality

Mind: the element of a person that enables him or her to be aware of the world and his or her experiences, to think, and to feel; the faculty of consciousness and thought

So, let's put this together...

I will love the Lord with the center and source of my thoughts and emotions, my innermost being. I will love the Lord with my moral and emotional nature as I identify myself as His creation, where He is the embodiment of my desire. I will love the Lord with an awareness of Him through the world He created and my interactions with the people He created for His glory.

In the second commandment, Jesus says to love your neighbor as yourself. A neighbor can be considered a friend or any other person you live with or have the chance to meet.[24] This would equate to everyone.

If you're thinking about what it means to love your neighbor as yourself, simply think about how you would like to be treated in a similar situation. In most situations, you want mercy, grace, an extra favor, help, support, good service, etc. You want people to care about you and help you when you need it most. This is your standard—giving others the same intense feeling of deep affection because it's what you would want.

CONCLUSION

I pray *Jump-Start Your Christian Life: Five Simple Ways to Refresh, Restore, and Reset* has not only encouraged you, but recharged your focus and resolve in godliness.

God has begun a good work in you.[25] He will provide you with everything you need in order to fulfill the purpose He has for you in this life, as He prepares you for eternity with Him.

Keep your focus on being a blessed person who lives for God's glory while praying to Him often in your delight of Him through your love for Him and others.

ENDNOTES

1. "G3306—menō—Strong's Greek Lexicon (KJV)." Blue Letter Bible. Accessed October 23, 2016. https://www.blueletterbible.org//lang/lexicon/lexicon.cfm?Strongs=G3306&t=KJV.

2. As you abide in Jesus, God will prune you. In gardening, pruning is important for improving or maintaining health, reducing risk, and both harvesting and increasing the yield or quality of flowers and fruits (https://en.wikipedia.org/wiki/Pruning). In like manner, God will remove and shape various parts of your life in order for you to be healthy and eliminate the risk of sin in your life so He can receive greater attention and glory as you display an obedient and faithful Christian life.

3. Ephesians 5:22–33.

4. Psalm 19:8, 119:105.

5. 2 Corinthians 6:14.

6. 1 Corinthians 15:33.

7. Ephesians 6:11–18.

8. Ephesians 4:29–32.

9. "G1391—*doxa*—Strong's Greek Lexicon (KJV)." Blue Letter Bible. Accessed January, 26, 2012. https://www.blueletterbible.org//lang/lexicon/lexicon.cfm?Strongs=G1391&t=KJV.

10. 1 Corinthians 6:19–20.

11. 2 Corinthians 5:20.

12. Luke 18:1–7; 1 Thessalonians 5:16–18.

13. Matthew 6:25–34.

14. Luke 17:20–21.

15. Jeremiah 31:31–34; Luke 17:20–21; John 14:26, 16:13.

16. 1 Corinthians 10:13.

17. John 17:15; 2 Thessalonians 3:1–3; 2 Timothy 4:18.

18. Genesis 2:29.

19. Genesis 2:8.

20. Genesis 2:25.

21. Genesis 2:16–17.

22. Genesis 3:1–6.

23. Satan is the first in recorded biblical history who sought to please himself. He sought to place himself above the stars of God and led over a third of the angels in heaven against God (Isaiah 14:12–15; Ezekiel 28:16–19; Luke 10:18; Revelation 12:4, 20).

24. "G4139—*plēsion*—Strong's Greek Lexicon (KJV)." Blue Letter Bible. Accessed February 5, 2012 https://www.blueletterbible.org//lang/lexicon/lexicon.cfm?Strongs=G4139&t=KJV.

25. Philippians 1:6.

(com)mission™

PUBLISHING

www.commissionpubs.com
info@commissionpubs.com

JUMP START YOUR CHRISTIAN LIFE

FIVE SIMPLE WAYS TO REFRESH RESTORE RESET

HAMP LEE III

(com)mission™ PUBLISHING

Jump-Start Your Christian Life: Five Simple Ways to Refresh, Restore, and Reset / Hamp Lee III—4th ed.

ISBN: 978-1-940042-37-4

CONTENTS

CONTENTS

www.ingramcontent.com/pod-product-compliance
Lightning Source LLC
Chambersburg PA
CBHW060546030426
42337CB00021B/4449